LIFESTYLE MASTERY MONEY MANAGEMENT
Eliminate Debt, Stop Impulse Spending, and Finance your Dreams

Jacob Fitzgerald

© **Copyright 2019 - All rights reserved.**

The contents of this book may not be reproduced, duplicated or transmitted without direct written permission from the author.

Under no circumstances will any legal responsibility or blame be held against the publisher for any reparation, damages, or monetary loss due to the information herein, either directly or indirectly.

Legal Notice:
This book is copyright protected. This is only for personal use. You cannot amend, distribute, sell, use, quote or paraphrase any part of the content within this book without the consent of the author.

Disclaimer Notice:
Please note the information contained within this document is for educational and entertainment purposes only. Every attempt has been made to provide accurate, up to date and reliable, complete information. No warranties of any kind are expressed or implied. Readers acknowledge that the author is not engaging in the rendering of legal, financial, medical or professional advice. The content of this book has been derived from various sources. Please consult a licensed professional before attempting any techniques outlined in this book.

By reading this document, the reader agrees that under no circumstances is the author responsible for any losses, direct or indirect, which are incurred as a result of the use of information contained within this document, including, but not limited to, —errors, omissions, or inaccuracies.

TABLE OF CONTENTS

Introduction

Chapter 1 – The Power of Good Financial Habits

Chapter 2 – The Importance of Budgeting

Chapter 3 – Top Causes of Ruined Budgets

Chapter 4 – Chronic Impulse Spending: A Deadly Adversary

Chapter 5 – Taking the Power Back from Chronic Impulse Spending

Chapter 6 – The Anatomy of Debt

Chapter 7 – How to Get Out of Debt

Conclusion

INTRODUCTION

Lifestyle mastery is made up of several important areas. One of the most important areas that every person needs to master is money management. Why?

Though money can't buy everything, it can make all things possible. Yes, money can't buy you love as the classic Beatles song goes. However, it can buy many of the things you'll need to be able to create environments or situations conducive to love such as regular family visits out of town, special gifts to your loved ones, and taking care of their needs, among others.

Money may not be able to buy you happiness, but it can help you afford the things that can make you happy! You can buy opportunities to experience awesome things like traveling all over the world, providing for your family, taking care of your parents in their sunset years, and buying your daughter that puppy she's been desperately asking you for the last few months, among others.

Make no mistake about it, money can be an important key to mastering and enjoying all other areas of your life.

This book is about mastering your personal finances, i.e., mastering money management. It's not a technical book, but it's a very practical one. In it, you'll understand 2 of the most important factors that can make or break your personal finances: debts and spending. The information you'll learn from this book doesn't require a degree in accounting or finance to understand. Any person who can read and write can understand the information presented in this book. That's why I believe that by the end of the book, you'll be ready to start managing your personal finances much better by managing your debts and spending much better.

If you're ready, turn the page and let's begin.

CHAPTER 1 – THE POWER OF GOOD FINANCIAL HABITS

Lifestyle mastery is really all about acquiring excellent habits. If you want to manage your health and fitness, then develop healthy eating and regular exercise habits. If you want to become the best basketball player in your team, then you should develop excellent training habits to develop your skills well. And when it comes to getting out or staying out of toxic debts and living a full and satisfying life, you'll need to develop excellent financial habits and avoid bad ones.

Bad habits can disrupt one's personal finances and keep a person from accomplishing his or her financial goals. But still, many people don't bother getting rid of them and replacing them with good ones. Why?

Generally speaking, there are 2 reasons for this: love of pleasure and fear of pain. Often times, bad habits are ways by which experience pleasure or avoid pain. Take for example taking drugs. It's a very dangerous and potentially fatal habit but why do junkies continue doing drugs? It's because of the massive pleasure they get from doing so. In fact, as they get acclimatized to the amount of drugs they use, the pleasure starts plateauing and they want to experience higher highs, which lead to increasing the amount of drugs used. Eventually, it can lead to overdose and in some cases, death.

An example of a bad habit that's driven by fear of pain is never going to the doctor for regular checkups out of fear that the doctor may diagnose the person with the same terminal illness that took away one of his or her parents. For that person, the possibility of being diagnosed with the same terminal illness evokes a strong emotion of fear because of seeing said parent writhe in agony with the sickness, which resulted in a slow and painful death.

How to Get Rid of Bad Habits

One of the most popular misconceptions about bad habits is that the best way to get rid of them is to just get rid of it or stop doing it. But human nature abhors a vacuum so when a person successfully removes a bad habit from his or her life and doesn't fill the void with a healthy one, the subconscious mind will find a way to fill up the void. It may do so by bringing back previous bad habits that were just stopped. Many times, those habits return worse than before.

So, how can you get rid of bad financial habits for good? You replace it with healthy ones.

When you focus on acquiring healthy financial habits instead of getting rid of unhealthy ones, you may be able to achieve 2 things. First, you will only have to do 1 thing instead of 2. Developing good habits that can eventually ease the bad ones out. You hit 2 birdies with one rock!

Second, you can minimize the chances of opening up a vacuum that the old habits or other bad habits can refill.

Here are other practical ways that you can get rid of bad financial habits.

<u>Plan Ahead</u>

If you want to optimize your chances of responding properly

when situations that can trigger your bad financial habits arise, you'll need to know beforehand how you should respond. If you wait until such situations arise before you think of how you should respond, it'd be too late. Believe me, you won't have time to even think.

By planning your course of action beforehand, you can quickly spring into action and either diffuse or escape those kinds of situations and minimize the risks of lingering too long. You already know the fire escape when a fire breaks out instead of having to figure it out while the fire's already burning and spreading quickly.

For example, think about what you should quickly do when you pass by a shop with items on display that triggers your desire for impulse buying? It may be to walk away as fast as you can and leave the mall quickly. It may be to give your wallet to your companion, who understands that he or she must keep it away from you at all costs every time you give it to him or her.

Identify and Cut the Triggers

Knowing that leaving the faucet on will flood your sink and eventually, flood the bathroom and your bedroom, I'm sure you'll make sure that the faucet's off before leaving. Knowing that your child has a severe allergy to shrimps, you'll do everything in your power to make sure she doesn't eat shrimp. If you know what triggers your bad financial habits, you can do the same: cut it off from the get-go. It's easier to run away from temptation than to fight it.

How can you identify your bad financial habit triggers? One of the best ways is keeping a journal. Write down how you felt or what happened before every occasion when you manifest your bad financial habits. You'll be surprised how helpful this can be.

Do you tend to gamble at the casino? What usually triggers it? Is it stress from work over very backlogs that urgently need to be finished? If so, then you can cut the trigger by figuring out ways to improve your personal productivity so that you can always finish your projects or work items on time or earlier. When you're able to find ways to do that, you can successfully disarm or cut your casino gambling trigger, as an example.

You can also minimize or disarm triggers by changing your environment, e.g., work, home, or commuting environment. This is because environment can have a great say on whether it'll be easier to keep bad financial habits and if developing or acquiring new and good ones will be harder.

For example, it will be hard for you to start developing the habit of investing in stocks or bonds when you're constantly surrounded by people who are very negative about investing. This is because we become who we spend a lot of time with regularly. Over time, their negative talk about investing will be able to program your mind that you shouldn't invest in stocks and bonds. This will also make it easier for you to keep all your savings in the bank, which isn't a healthy financial habit to have. It's because if you don't invest a good portion of your savings, inflation will weaken its purchasing power and make it insufficient for your future needs.

Ask for Help

Especially for deeply ingrained ones, getting help from other people is a crucial aspect of overcoming bad habits. Rare are the people who are able to overcome their obesity, smoking, work, or relationship problems on their own. Enlisting the help of another person can help you bear the burden of successfully kicking bad habits.

How do you enlist other people's help? One of the easiest ways to do that is by reading books of experts on personal finance like Dave Ramsey and Suze Orman or enrolling in personal finance workshops and seminars. But if you personally know someone who has very good financial habits, which you can tell by their financial situation, then ask to be mentored by that person and hang out with him or her more often.

Another way to enlist the help of other people is to designate one or two people to be your financial habits accountability partner. Give these people authority to penalize you in whatever manner they deem fit should you backslide into your bad financial habits or if you fail to develop new and healthy financial habits. It can give you motivation to really do your best knowing that if you fail, you'll be held accountable by someone and be penalized for such failures.

Lastly, you can enlist the help of others by joining a personal finance advocacy group or club. Why? These are good places to find people who are also taking the same journey as you are. By hooking up with them, you'll be able to walk the journey of overcoming bad financial habits through developing good ones with other people, which can be very encouraging.

<u>Watch Your Words</u>

Negative self-talk is a very subtle negative habit that can severely impact your ability to get rid of bad financial habits. Why? The words you constantly speak to yourself or think in your conscious mind will program your subconscious mind, which is the driving force behind your habits.

If you always say:

- You're a very undisciplined person whenever you slip up and fail to set aside money for savings, then your subconscious mind will continuously find ways to make you spend all your monthly income so that you won't have any savings left at the end of the month;
- You're never going to overcome your casino gambling habits whenever you slip and throw away money in a casino, your subconscious mind will always find ways for you to

come back to gambling in casinos; and
- You're an impulsive shopaholic and you give in to the temptation to buy something that's not in your budget, your subconscious mind will always find ways to make sure you continue to buy on impulse.

Instead of saying or thinking those things, you can add a "but" statement at the end to neutralize the negativity and program your mind to do the opposite. To use the 3 examples above:

- "I'm am extremely undisciplined person BUT I'm already working on this and it's just a matter of time before I get this down to pat!"
- "I currently feel that I won't be able to overcome this casino gambling habit, BUT I know that I will be able to overcome this eventually."
- "I'm an impulsive shopaholic, BUT because I'm committed to changing, I won't be for long."

Instead of being hard on yourself and beating yourself up whenever you revert to old financial habits, just acknowledge your mistake, learn what led you to committing it, learn from it, and move forward. Moping and pitying yourself will keep you from overcoming bad financial habits but moving forward with a realistic hope can help you overcome them.

Good Financial Habits to Develop

We've talked about some of the worst financial habits that can keep you from mastering the financial aspect of your lifestyle. And now, we'll talk about some of the best financial habits you should consider acquiring to allow you to take control of your personal finances. Just keep in mind that I've presented them in no particular order.

Automatic Savings

Of all the important financial habits that you must learn to develop, consistently putting aside money for savings should be top priority. This is especially important if you don't have an adequate emergency fund established yet. Consider this the first "bill" you'll need to pay every month.

If you want to ensure that saving money truly becomes automatic, open another savings or checking account to which you can automatically transfer savings money from your payroll or primary bank account. Set the account such that it will automatically transfer a fixed amount of savings to your second account.

Record All Your Expenses

When you record all your expenses, you put yourself in a position to see clearly where your money goes. You'll be able to get an average of your monthly expenses per category, which will allow you to create a more realistic budget. And if you record them on a spreadsheet like Google Sheets, Excel, or Numbers, it will be very easy for you to perform mathematical operations on your expense details such as sub-totaling per category, sub-totaling per month, and computing average expenses per category per month, among others. If you're more technical, you can even compute for standard deviation, i.e., by how much your actual expenses exceed or fall short of the average estimate.

Let me share with you my personal experience of how helpful recording expenses on a spreadsheet can be. Several years ago, I was at a loss on how my bank account decreased by a significant amount. I didn't recall spending for something major during that time period, but fortunately, I recorded all my expenses in an Excel spreadsheet.

Using Excel's statistical function, I was able to easily sort my expenses for that time period according to category and within each category, the exact expense items. Lo and behold, the reason why my bank account's balance dipped significantly was because of numerous small-ticket items that are negligible individually but when totaled, amounted to a significant amount. When I became aware that small-ticket expenses can become one big amount if not I'm not cognizant about them, I was able to prevent similar accumulations of small ticket items. In turn, it helped me control my finances much better.

<u>Prepare for Tomorrow</u>

It's easy to take future financial needs for granted during youth. It's probably because retirement is so far away and the chances of getting sick or getting into an accident seem to be very, very low when one is young and just starting out. But the best time to prepare tomorrow isn't tomorrow but today. Why?

If you put aside and invest money now to have a specific amount for your retirement, you can afford to make smaller but regular investment amounts. But if you decide to start preparing for your retirement 20 years later, you'll need to regularly put in a much higher amount of money just to have the same amount for retirement. This is because given the same average annual rate of return on investments and the same target amount of money for the future, the longer the investment period, the smaller the amount of money that needs to be invested and vice-versa. So, start saving and investing as soon as possible.

Another way you should consider preparing for the future is by getting life and health insurance. Life is full of risks and you'll never know when you'll get into an accident or acquire a potentially fatal illness. With insurance, you pay a relatively smaller amount (premiums) that will provide you (or your surviving) family members a much bigger amount of money in case something bad happens to you.

Many people go bankrupt because of a single tragic incident that limits their ability to earn income and eats up their savings, if any. Insurance can help you defray those costs without touching your savings.

Use Debts Wisely

I'm not in favor of how many personal finance gurus demonize debts. However, I'm also not advocating it completely. For me, one of the important habits to have is using debt wisely. When used wisely, it can be a very good personal finance ally. If used unwisely, however, it can lead to financial ruin.

So how do you use debts wisely? When should you take on debt and when shouldn't you? Well, discuss it in more detail in Chapter 6: The Anatomy of Debt.

Use Envelopes

The envelope system of budgeting involves assigning an envelope for each of your expense categories, e.g., house food, utilities, transportation, recreation, etc. Then, fill each envelope with an amount of money that's based on your estimated monthly category expenses.

This can be a very practical way of monitoring your expenses for the month. Whenever you withdraw money from an envelope, you become aware how much is left for the month. And when you're aware, you can manage your budget accordingly. It's also a very good way to limit your expenses for each category because you'll be limited by the amount of money in each envelope.

Continuous Learning

This particular habit is one that you should have for all areas of your life because it will ensure you continue improving in them. For money management mastery, reading personal finance and psychology-related books and blogs, watching instructional videos on said topics, and attending seminars and workshops can help you continuously grow in knowledge and wisdom when it comes to managing your money well.

Bad Financial Habits to Break

Some of the worse financial habits that you'll need to break if you want to achieve complete mastery over your finances are:

- Paying bills late because more than just incurring penalties and charges, your credit scores can be negatively affected too;
- Paying only the minimum amount due on your credit card balance because it will just maintain the total amount you owe and worse, you'll end up paying so much more for your debts over the long term;
- Impulse buying or spending money mindlessly can keep you from meeting your real needs because the funds you could've used for them can go to things that aren't needed or important;
- Keeping subscriptions that you no longer use, which can be a substantial money drain;
- Eating out every day, because food from commercial establishments costs at least twice compared to eating food prepared at home;
- Procrastinating on saving money and investments because as mentioned earlier, the earlier you start, the less amount you'll need to save and invest regularly and the bigger the amount you can have in the future;
- Spending more than you make every month;
- Touching your savings and investment funds;
- Saving "leftover" money instead of spending "leftover" money, i.e., money remaining after deducting money for savings; and
- Not getting insurance.

CHAPTER 2 – THE IMPORTANCE OF BUDGETING

If there's anything that will help you to really master your lifestyle, particularly your relationship with money, it's budgeting. Many people usually react in a very negative way when they hear the word "budget" because, in their minds, it's all about limitations, restrictions, and a life of pure misery. Or they think that they make too little income that budgeting isn't applicable to them, i.e., you can't budget something so small as to be "unbudgetable."

The truth, however, budgeting is neither as impossible as many people think it is nor is it applicable only to the rich with so much money to budget. In fact, there's very little need to budget money if one is swimming in a whole lot of cash compared to one who has very limited money.

Budgeting may be considered as a keystone skill, i.e., a skill that once learned automatically leads to mastering other skills or experiencing multiple benefits. That's why if you master it, you may be able to master other important areas of your lifestyle.

In particular, here are some of the best reasons why you should learn the all-important skill of budgeting.

Budgeting Minimizes Risk of Overspending

Many people who are mired in toxic personal debts became so because of chronic and severe overspending. Every month, expenses always exceed income. This normal occurrence has wreaked havoc in their personal finances as evidenced by being buried in a pile of bad and costly debts. It can do the same to you in the long run.

Many people who shun the budgeting practice for fear of being restricted in their spending end up being restricted anyway by something that doesn't give any satisfaction or utility: debt payments. Once buried in so much debt and being hounded by creditors, their lives become more and more affected or even controlled by the latter in ways that aren't just financial. Many debt-ridden folks are severely stressed both financially and emotionally.

Mastering the skill of budgeting can help you avoid the same fate as such people have already had. Or if you're already one of them, budgeting can help you change your fate, i.e., get out of debt.

Budgeting Can Help You Achieve Your Dreams and Goals

Failing to plan – as the cliché goes – is planning to fail. If you plan, your chances of failing are much, much lower than if you didn't plan. When it comes to your life dreams and goals, you can't afford to have a plan.

Since a budget is a financial plan that can help you spend wisely, having one and sticking to it can help you focus the money that you earn on your important life dreams and goals. And when you're able to focus on those, your chances of being able to accomplish or achieve them are much higher. While money can't buy everything, it can buy things that can help you accomplish anything.

Budgeting Can Help You Set Aside Money for the Future

When you don't have a budget, your chances of being able to save money on a regular basis are practically nil. Or even if you're able to save money without having a budget, the amount you'll be able to save will most probably be much lower.

Budgeting can help you consistently save money by making savings a habit and by minimizing your risks for spending your savings money. Over the long haul, it can help you create, grow, and protect wealth for your future needs and wants particularly retirement.

Budgeting Can Buy You Peace of Mind

For many people who refuse to budget their money, their number one objection is they don't like to feel "controlled" or "restricted." They only find out later on – often when it's too late – that by foregoing the budgeting process earlier in life, their financial circumstances will eventually control or restrict the way they live their lives. Often the control is not a pleasant one.

When you budget your money, it's actually you who has the control or the power over your money. And over time, budgeting can also give you a great sense of control over your financial destiny. When you're able to control your financial destiny, you'll be able to live a financial worry-free life because you don't have to worry how you can continue affording the lifestyle you're currently living or how you can accomplish your life dreams and goals.

Budgeting isn't about restricting your ability to live a full and satisfying life. To the contrary, it's something that can help you do it by ensuring that you'll eventually have enough money to live such kind of a life.

Budgeting Can Help Improve Your Financial Flexibility

Contrary to what many people think about budgeting being a very restrictive and stiff practice, it can actually be flexible. This is because you hold the power to move your funds in between categories within the month as necessary. If your car needs to be repaired this month, you can – through budgeting – shift some funds away from recreation expenses to the needed repairs, as an example.

But still, the general idea of budgeting is grounded on some level of restriction. If it's too "flexible," it won't work. If it's too restrictive, it's not good either. The general idea is be as unyielding as you can be in terms of saving money and keeping it untouched while giving some leeway for occasional changes in spending amounts for certain categories when needed.

With budgeting you can have flexibility in spending categories and when you're able to successfully build up enough wealth, you can enjoy financial flexibility.

Budgeting Provides Financial Control

If you feel like your personal finances are all over the place and if you frequently think about where your monthly income is actually spent on, budgeting can help you put these to rest. This is because budgeting involves monitoring and controlling of your finances, which can let you take the necessary actions as needed. And if you're able to prepare and implement a very good budget consistently, your chances of being able to fund your life goals and dreams can be much higher. Budgeting can help you take the wheel of your financial destiny.

CHAPTER 3 – TOP CAUSES OF RUINED BUDGETS

It's one thing to create a very good and sensible budget, but that's only half the battle. As with any battle worth fighting, the other half of winning it involves effectively executing the plan or the budget. And when it comes to successfully implementing your budget, you'll need to be wary of the top reasons why many Americans fail to do so or worse, why their budgets were completely ruined. When you know these traps, you can avoid them.

Ignorance of Other Opportunities

Ours is a world where resources are scarce. This means we normally have to give up something in order to get another. When we choose to buy something, the money we use to buy that thing can no longer be used to buy something else. This means that in everything we do or buy, there's an opportunity cost.

Ignorance of opportunity costs can trip people up in their budgets because they only see the shiny side of purchases to the exclusion of the not-so-shiny side. Opportunity costs is normally represented by other alternatives.

Take for example buying a car on loan, which will require making monthly amortizations. When taking that kind of financial obligation, we are effectively closing the doors to other opportunities depending on our monthly income and budget. These could mean giving up monthly out-of-town trips with our spouse and kids or building up our emergency fund in case we don't have one yet. Awareness of such costs can minimize risks for making purchases outside of the planned budget because you know what it can really cost you.

Mental Accounting

This refers to a person's tendency to segregate his or her money into different mental accounts like recreation, house food, clothes, work travel expenses, etc. Under this scenario, a person's ability or tendency to spend is "restricted" by each account's amount. At first glance, this is what budgeting should really be about, right? Well, not really.

You see, mental accounting only takes into consideration the opportunity costs associated with a particular account instead of the entire picture. And this can render a person's budget inflexible and to a certain extent, ineffective. Allow me to illustrate.

Let's say that I received a $1,000 birthday gift from my Mom, which in my mind was already budgeted under the "recreation" account to celebrate my special day 3 days later. But on my way to work the 2 days before my planned celebration, my car's rear left tire blew out because the treads were practically wiped out. Therefore, I had to buy a new pair of tires, which I currently have no money for.

Because I have already budgeted my Mom's $1,000 birthday gift under my mental recreation account, I'm having second thoughts using a good portion of it to buy new tires even if I needed to. Why? It's because of my strict and inflexible mental accounting.

If I end up not buying new tires just so I can use the entire $1,000 gift to celebrate my special day, I will have a hard time getting around in the next few weeks or months until I'm able to save up for a new pair of tires. I may even end up spending more money and ruining my budget because I'll have to take the cab or Uber just to get around, which is more expensive than simply driving my car. In this case, will a day of celebrating my birthday exactly the way I planned be worth the weeks of commuting inconvenience and bigger expenses? I don't think so.

In that example, my being anal about mental accounting would have resulted in less personal productivity, bigger expenses, and more stress over the next several weeks due to not being able to drive. If I had insisted on keeping my mental budget for recreation to the neglect of an unexpected need, I sacrificed the bigger picture for a small portion of it.

Not that I'm saying mental accounting is bad. It's not, ok? I'm just saying that if done in a very rigid and extreme fashion without taking into consideration the bigger picture of life, then it can actually ruin one's budget and personal productivity.

"Special" Occasions

While special occasions are worth celebrating, there are 2 things that should be considered: what should really be counted as "special" and the tendency to go overboard.

One of the ways special occasions can wreak havoc on our budget is when we aren't able to limit the number of "special" occasions worth celebrating in our lives. As such, it can be very easy to go beyond our budgetary limits. Even seemingly small expenses associated with such celebrations can add up to substantial amounts that can substantially impact our monthly or even annual budgets. To this extent, it's worth setting strict criteria for qualifying occasions as special enough to spend on. Annual anniversaries can be worth celebrating but "month"-saries? C'mon!

Another way special occasions can wreak havoc on our budgets is when we don't set a budget for them! Even if we limit the number of special occasions to only 2, we can still go overboard when our spending limit's sky's-the-limit. To minimize this risk, it's also important to set spending limits for each special occasion worth celebrating.

Bias for the Moment

This is more commonly known as the tendency to pursue instant gratification at the expense of better rewards in the future or more important things for the future. In short, this is the tendency to favor immediate benefits and rewards over future ones.

A good example of how this type of tendency can negatively impact one's budget is choosing to buy a new car on mortgage, even if the currently-owned car is still working generally well, instead of building up an emergency fund or contributing to one's IRA or 401(k). If income is limited such that only one of the 2 is possible, going for the immediate reward of driving a brand-new car on mortgage can severely limit or even completely prevent putting up an emergency fund or saving for retirement, both of which are far more important than the fleeting feeling of driving a brand-new car.

What makes this such a dangerous budget adversary is that it can be a very powerful emotion that overrides any sense of logic. The fact that many people do this because of inability to delay gratification is a testament to its strong power to lead to financial ruin.

Virtual Vs. Actual Money

The bias for the moment can also lead to another potentially budget-dangerous habit, which is bias for virtual money over actual money. And by this, I refer to the preference to pay via credit card over paying with cold, hard cash.

According to a 2017 study by Ariely and Kreisler, paying with cold, hard cash can feel more painful compared to using credit cards. This means paying with credit cards is much easier and is painless, which makes it easier to choose this mode of payment. But how can virtual money be dangerous for one's financial health?

One principle that explains why many people find it hard to change bad and currently painful habits is that the pain associated with ditching such habits is perceived to be much greater than the pain they currently bring. In short, it's all about choosing the lesser evil, i.e., the alternative with the lesser pain.

The thing about using credit cards is that it allows for the segregation of the pleasure of buying stuff from the pain of paying for them, at least for the moment. But the seemingly short separation time may be considered an eternity such that it can make a person focus too much on the current pleasure because the pain is delayed. With no current pain, current pleasure wins and often results in overspending via credit cards.

Now, I'm not saying using credit cards is akin to selling one's financial soul to the financial devil. The point here is that unless a person is not a shopaholic or an impulsive shopper, using virtual money over actual money can lead to ruined budgets.

The "Might-As-Well" Mentality

Being a perfectionist when it comes to budgeting isn't a healthy approach to budgeting. But equally unhealthy is the lenient "might-as-well" mentality to it.

The "might-as-well" mentality – referred to as the "what-the-hell" mentality in a 2010 study by Herman and Polivy – is one that causes even more indulgence after feeling like such a failure during minor lapses in judgment. A good example would be: "Man, I've really blown my recreational budget for this month. Might as well go all the way since I've ruined it already and there's no point in keeping the budget."

Depleted Willpower Reserves

Contrary to popular opinion, willpower isn't an infinite resource. It's a finite one. Much like a person gets tired after exercising for extended periods of time, a person can also mentally get tired and become weak at controlling him or herself after using willpower throughout a period of time.

As with any bad habit, it's hard to resist overspending when one's will power reserves are very low or almost depleted. It's like asking someone to lift a pair of dumbbells after performing 100 straight repetitions to failure. When willpower is depleted, it's very easy for impulses, cravings, urges, and desires to override the mind and hijack the wallet.

Therefore, it's best to avoid situations where the propensity to act in ways that can ruin or compromise budgets when willpower is very low, such as the end of a very long and stressful day at work or when in an emotionally tiring situation.

Therapeutic Shopping

According to Cryder et al. (2008), many people admit to using shopping as a form of therapy, i.e., retail therapy. This happens when people experience negative emotions that compel them to get a quick shot of positive feelings. This isn't surprising because as mentioned earlier, willpower reserves can be very low during or after highly emotional incidents, which makes the temptation to spend beyond one's budget very strong. Retail therapy, in particular, helps people who are going through "down" moments see themselves in a much better situation than the one they're currently in. For many people, buying new things – especially things they like – give them a shot of happy hormones, hence the strong tendency to handle negative feelings through shopping.

Buying Addiction

According to a 2007 published study in World Psychiatry by D.W. Black entitled A Review of Compulsive Buying Disorder, about 6% of the American population may be considered as compulsive buyers suffering from a condition called shopping addiction. According to Black, this condition is considered to be an impulse-control disorder, the degrees of which vary within a continuum.

Some people simply shop too much, but some people are over-the-top when it comes to shopping because they're compulsive shoppers. Most of the time, the buy so many things, most of which they neither need nor can afford. And in many cases, this disorder doesn't just wreak havoc on their personal finances and lead to bankruptcy but can also jeopardize their mental health and their most important relationships.

The first crucial thing to do to address this kind of disorder is to seek professional treatment. Doing so will allow you to discover the underlying reason for compulsive shopping and how it developed. Often times, journaling is an integral part of therapy for this disorder because it helps recovering compulsive shoppers, a.k.a., shopaholics, to discover behavioral triggers so they can avoid those triggers.

Lack of Accountability

Often times, people are troubled with defending their choices to others and to themselves. While making sense of things is a basic human motivation, it's not the same as being right, according to T.D. Wilson, in his 2011 published book Redirect: The Surprising New Science of Psychological Change.

A very good example of this as it relates to exceeding one's budget is buying something that's neither needed nor beneficial like another pair of sneakers. Even if the buyer already has 2 good pairs of sneakers on hand and the price of the pair of sneakers in question will make him exceed his budget for that month, he will still buy the pair and justify his actions by saying to himself or the person he's accountable to things like:

- "It was on sale at 90% discount! I saved 90% by buying it now instead of before the price drop!"
- "What are the chances that this particular sneaker

model, which I've been praying for in the last 6 months ago, would drop its price by 90%? Practically zero and as such, this being on sale at 90% off is a sign from the heavens that God wants me to have this pair. How can I disobey God's will for my life?"

A person who refuses to take accountability for his budget and always shifts the blame on events, circumstances, other people, and even God is a person whose budget will always be ruined.

CHAPTER 4 – CHRONIC IMPULSE SPENDING: A DEADLY ADVERSARY

Of the many threats to effective budgeting, nothing beats chronic impulse spending. At some point, all of us fell under the spell of this enchanting thing. We saw something in the store that really tugged at our hearts – and wallets – and when we bought the thing, we got a strong shot of excitement and thrill. On our way home, we may have justified our giddiness at trying that thing out as soon as we get home by thinking of many different ways that it can really make a difference in our lives.

However, that thing wasn't something we really needed or intended to buy in the first place. We just had that strong impulse to buy it at that moment. Our emotions hijacked our brain in order to hijack our wallet.

Impulse buying is something that many people fall prey to. It doesn't matter how frugal a person is because the impulse can be very strong at times that it's practically impossible to resist. And the worst part of impulse buying is that it can significantly impact a person's short-term finances while keeping that person from developing other sound financial habits that can foster financial security and prosperity over the long haul.

It's important for us to be aware of our impulse buying tendencies so we can identify and take necessary steps to nip this problem in the bud. When we're able to do that, we can make better financial decisions more regularly.

Let's clarify something before proceeding though: impulse buying in and by itself isn't evil. If done responsibly once in a while, it can be a very good motivational tool as it can be a way to reward ourselves after accomplishing something difficult or consoling ourselves every now and then after going through very trying times in our lives. However, impulse buying is like a very sharp set of kitchen knives that should be used with utmost care because if handled improperly, it can cause a lot of damage.

But really, what is impulse buying? It's basically an unplanned buying decision, i.e., out of the blue or spontaneous buying. People who are frequently buy things on impulse are referred to as – surprise, surprise – impulse buyers.

Drivers of Chronic Impulse Buying

One of the most important things that can help overcome impulse buying is awareness of the triggers or drivers of such behavior. We can't address a problematic situation that we aren't aware of so to help you understand impulse buying better, here are some of impulse buying's most powerful drivers.

Shopping Addiction

Most people feel a momentary "high" when buying or getting something new. The excitement escalates as they start using or experiencing the new thing. This is because novelty is one of the things that fascinate people and acquiring or experiencing new things help trigger the release of a happy hormone called dopamine, which makes people feel, well, happy! And the mere thought or anticipation of getting or experiencing something new can make most people's brain release dopamine and produce a "high" or "feel good" effect.

FOMO or Fear of Missing Out

Human nature makes us want to have beautiful things that others have. It also makes us want to experience the same or very similar things as our colleagues, friends, or relatives do. It's these tendencies that can cause us to buy things that we don't really intend to buy or need at the moment. The fear of missing out on things that others are enjoying is one major factor for impulse spending.

Erroneous Ideas

As we learned earlier, one of the most common excuses of compulsive buyers who splurge money away during sales is the idea of saving money buying something with a heavily marked-down price. If a particular item on sale used to sell for $100 and is now on sale at only $30, the logic goes that buying it now will make you save $70!

This logic will hold true if the item in question is something we really need or have already budgeted for. But if it was something we neither needed nor budgeted for, it's wrong to say we saved $70 by buying it. The truth is we spent $30 more than we should have in our budget.

Why it's a Problem

Chronic impulse buying always disrupts any person's budget and puts that person at high risk for not being able to save money for future needs. It can be very easy – and unconscious – to spend money that's originally budgeted for something important on things that are neither needed nor budgeted for. Over time, this can result in lack of funds for the things that you really need. Worse, chronic impulse buying can keep a person from developing financial habits that are crucial for long-term financial security and prosperity.

There's a principle in the Bible that says "Start children off on the way they should go, and even when they are old they will not turn from it." The idea behind it is that the earlier a person learns and does something on a regular basis, the higher the chances that he or she will stick to it over the long haul. The longer a person stays a chronic impulse buyer, the higher the chances that the habit will stick and eventually wreak havoc in his or her personal finances.

This is the power of chronic impulse spending. This is what makes it a potent adversary that must be dealt with by anybody who'd want to master their lifestyle through money management.

CHAPTER 5 – TAKING THE POWER BACK FROM CHRONIC IMPULSE SPENDING

While chronic impulse spending is a sly but strong adversary, it's one that can be overcome with the right strategies and proper implementation of such strategies. The following are practical things you can do that can help you keep chronic impulse spending in check.

Create a Realistic Budget and Implement It

Sorry, but there's no going around this but you will need to have a budget and faithfully adhere to it. Failing to plan is planning to fail and when you make a budget, you prepare a financial plan that can help you manage your finances well.

However, it's not a magic pill that once you pop, makes everything in your personal finances fine and dandy. The other half of effective budgeting is sticking to your budget, i.e., implementing it. A budget without action is merely wishful thinking. A budget acted on faithfully is what can help you manage your personal finances very well.

Reward Yourself Responsibly

Chronic impulsive spending may be considered a motivational

issue in that there are certain motivations – or triggers – that prompt the behavior. And according to one of the greatest self-help experts of all time, Tony Robbins, there are only two major motivations for the things people do: desire for pleasure and the fear of pain.

Chronic impulsive spending is driven by either or both. And more a person feels deprived of pleasure or the longer he or she experiences "pain" from complete deprivation, the stronger the desire for that which is deprived becomes. It can reach the point where willpower reserves aren't enough to hold a person back anymore.

When you reward yourself every now and then, and within reasonable limits, you'll be able to do 2 things. First, you'll be able to give yourself something to look forward to when doing something challenging, such as controlling the impulse to buy things on the spot. Second, you'll be like a pressure cooker that is able to release excess steam and prevent the pressure from becoming too strong to the point that the cooker can explode. By rewarding yourself regularly and responsibly, you can better manage your buying impulses.

Wait for a While

When you give yourself at least overnight before buying something you impulsively want to buy, you can create a wide enough chasm between your emotions and the purchase, which minimizes the risk for impulse buying.

Impulse buying tendencies are at its highest when time is very short, and emotions are very strong. When you give yourself at least overnight before buying things that you strongly wanted to buy on impulse, you'll find that your initial emotions would've subsided enough to the point that the desire to buy something goes away. There's a saying that never say or do something at the height of your emotions because often times, you'll regret it once the emotions subside. Chronic impulsive buying is a very good example of such a situation.

Give yourself at least 24 hours before deciding to buy something "impulsively." Chances are, you won't want to pursue it anymore after letting enough time pass you by.

Planned Shopping

Before you go shopping or even do the groceries, list down the things that you really plan to buy. Having a list ready will allow you to shop or do your groceries as fast as possible, which minimizes your risks for impulsive buying. When you don't have a list and think about what you really need or want to buy, you put yourself in a very vulnerable position for impulsive buying because you'll expose yourself longer to the shopping-inducing environment that most supermarkets and department stores purposefully cultivate.

Don't Bring Your Kids Along

Nothing can compel or pressure you to spend for something outside of your budget than a child who sees something he or she likes and throws a very loud tantrum in public. The best offense is good defense and in this case, prevention is the best defense. When you don't bring your child along for grocery shopping, you eliminate all risks of being emotionally blackmailed into indulging your child's impulsive desire to get stuff and throw tantrums.

Manage Your Email Lists Well

Joining a lot of email lists puts you at risk of impulsive buying too. Why? Internet marketers are very good salespeople who write very good sales copy intended to make people buy stuff even if they don't need it. If you joined a lot of email lists, you may do well to unsubscribe from most if not all of them to minimize temptations for impulse online buying.

If you really think you're better off staying with those lists, then the least you can do is to separate the emails from your friendly neighborhood internet marketers from your personal ones. The best approach you can take is to create a separate email address specifically just for emails from internet marketers. That way, you can minimize risks for impulsive buying even if you're actively glued to your personal or work emails.

Bring Money Only When You Shop

Remember how we talked about how much easier it is to buy stuff using a credit card instead of cold, hard cash? When you just bring slightly more than enough money than you estimate your planned purchases will cost, you're effectively putting hedges around you to keep you from impulsively buying stuff even if you wanted to. This means you may need to leave your ATM card at home too just to ensure you don't have the means to buy more than what you really budgeted for at the mall or the grocery.

Make a Waiting List for Major Purchases

Whenever you feel the strong urge to buy something with a relatively heavy price tag such as a top-of-the-line smartphone, a big-ass smart TV, or a major car accessory, list it down on a physical or digital list. Make sure to include the name of the item, the store from which you saw it, the price of the item, and the date when you first saw it and had the urge to buy it.

Once you've recorded it in your list, commit to postponing the purchase for 30 days, hence the need to record the date. Once the 30-day postponement period's over, check yourself to see how much you still want that item. If you still feel that the item will be really beneficial for you, then go ahead and buy it. But chances are high that by the time the 30th day rolls in, your initial desire to spend that much money on that item has greatly waned. If so, then delete it from the list and forget the item.

Lead Yourself Not into Temptation...

One of the best strategies to overcome a problematic habit is to avoid circumstances and environments that can make it very tempting and easy to indulge in that habit. When it comes to shopping, the most tempting situations and locations are malls, shops, supermarkets, or any shopping places.

The best way to not lose against an enemy is to avoid getting into a fight with it. So, do as the Lord's Prayer asks from God the Father: lead us (or yourself) not into temptation but deliver us (or yourself) from (impulse buying) evil.

Oh, the same goes for online shopping websites like Amazon.com and e-Bay for physical products and JVZoo, ClickBank, or Warrior Plus for digital products. In fact, it can even be much easier to fall into temptation in these websites because unlike physical stores, you can easily access these anytime and anywhere in the world that has Internet.

If you must, have a trusted friend install site blocking apps on your phone and computer to help you stay off such sites regardless of how tempted you are to do so. By having another person set up the site-blocking apps, only he or she can change the settings, so you won't be able to unblock shopping sites.

Practice Mindfulness Meditation

What's meditation got to do with curbing chronic impulse buying? Well, a lot!

You see, one of the most important keys to overcoming chronic impulsive buying is awareness of the habit as it starts to manifest. Chronic impulse buying is a compulsion, which is often carried out unconsciously. Awareness and regret usually come when it's too late and the purchase is already done. But if you become aware the moment the impulse buying urge appears, you can stop the impulse dead in its tracks either by postponing it or ditching it completely.

A very simple and doable mindfulness meditation practice is the box-breathing technique, which bestselling author and former Navy SEAL Mark Divine taught in his book The Way of the SEAL. This technique involves breathing cycles that are made up of 4 equal-duration steps. These steps are:

1. Breathing deeply for 5 seconds;
2. Holding the breath for 5 seconds;
3. Exhaling completely for 5 seconds; and
4. Holding the exhaled breath for 5 seconds.

The key to this technique is focusing your attention on your breath, i.e., the duration and the action. Doing it every day for at least 10 minutes will help you become more aware of how you breathe and improve your focus.

Over time, such awareness will extend to your emotions and the things you do, including impulsive buying. And when you become more aware of it, you'll be in a much better position to stop it dead in its tracks because it's easier to stop an enemy you're aware of than one that you're not.

Know Your Priorities

It's easy to spend recklessly and impulsively when you're not aware of your priorities. It's like trying to run on a treadmill. Why? Impulsive buying is an unconscious attempt at filling a need or a purpose. But when you're not aware of your priorities or what truly important to you, your actions will be random and meaningless, and you'll continue doing them thinking it's really helping you achieve your goals and priorities in life. But because they don't, it can be easy to believe that perhaps, more impulsive spending will do the trick. It can be a vicious downward spiral of financial death.

When you know your priorities, it will be much easier for you to curb your impulse spending habit. How? When you chance upon something in stores that triggers your impulse to buy it, ask yourself how is this relevant to achieving your life goals and taking care of your top priorities in life? If you can't answer it quickly and clearly, you'll have a compelling reason not to proceed with the impulsive purchase. It can help make you aware that if you proceed, you'll just be wasting money that could've otherwise been used to achieve your goals and take care of your priorities in life.

CHAPTER 6 – THE ANATOMY OF DEBT

We hear and read so much about millions of Americans wallowing in a sea of debts, barely getting by and making ends meet. So much that in the eyes of millions of Americans, and people all over the world, debt is the reincarnation of the devil himself. If debt were a person, he or she would cry "foul" and "I'm innocent until proven guilty and not guilty until proven innocent!"

Don't get me wrong now. I'm neither playing as the devil's advocate nor promoting debt. What I want to establish early in this book is the right awareness of and mindset about personal debts. While it's true that it can really ruin a person's financial and personal life, it also has the potential to make that person's life much more beautiful. So, my goal here is to give you the real score about debt.

What is Debt?

For purposes of personal financial management, debt refers to any sum of money a person owes and is legally obligated to pay others. The key word here is "obligated," which implies that it must be paid at a specific time and under specific terms. Many personal finance experts qualify debts even further as money already due to be paid back to a creditor. Based on such a definition, utility and credit card bills whose due dates haven't arrived yet aren't considered debts yet but as expenses or payables.

Bottom line: debt is money you are obligated to pay now or at a specific time in the future.

The Cost of Debt

When you buy an iPhone, the price at which you do includes the costs of making the phone (including research and development), marketing it, and a nice profit margin for the stockholders of Apple, Inc. When you buy 2 pounds of beef from your favorite local butcher, the price at which you do includes the costs of raising cattle, delivering it to your butcher, storage, and your favorite local butcher's profit.

You see: anything of value has a cost. You pay money to compensate the people or business who provides you with certain benefits, be it the use of a sleek and sexy smartphone (Apple) or eating a delicious chunk of steak (your butcher). It has to be a win-win situation, i.e., you get what you want or need and the providing party earns money to continue living and operating as a business.

The cost of buying things is called price. The cost of enlisting services of professionals is called professional fee or service fee. The cost of borrowing money – or debt – is called interest.

Why do you need to pay interest on your debts? Do your creditors deserve it? Is it evil or immoral to charge interest?

To answer the first question, it's because you need to. Creditors – the people who lend you money – are allowed to charge you reasonable interest under the law.

To answer the second question, yes, they deserve it. Why? Hadn't they given you their money for you to use, they could've used it in other ways that can earn them more money like starting a business or adding more capital to an existing business. By lending you their money, they've foregone the opportunity to earn money as well. By paying interest, you make it worth their while to lend you their money. And if you're an entrepreneur, you'd perfectly understand this logic.

To answer the third question, it depends. For Muslims, yes, it is, according to the Quran. That's why there's such a thing as Islamic Banking, where loans are packaged in a way that they're not "loans" and interest isn't packaged as interest as we know it. For non-Muslims it's subjective according to the rate of interest charged. Excessive interest rates are usually frowned upon as "usurious" or "immoral," especially if levied upon people or small businesses that are barely getting by. Even the criteria for "excessive" is subjective, depending on who you talk to.

Interest is the creditors – the person or institution lending the money – profit. If the cost of making an iPhone is $100 and Apple sells it for $2,000, the profit is $1,900, which is Apple's acceptable compensation for providing people with the phone. For creditors, the interest is their compensation for taking the risk to lend money to others who may or may not pay them back.

The amount of interest you will need to pay is dependent on 3 factors: the principal amount owed, how long will you pay off the debt (tenor), and the interest rate. Assuming the same principal balance and tenor, the higher the interest rate, the higher the interest you'll have to pay. Assuming the same principal balance and interest rate, the longer the tenor, the higher the total interest payments will be, but the monthly interest will be smaller.

Amortization Payments

This is what will determine whether or not you can afford to take on debt. As a rule of thumb, the amount of regular amortization payments you will be obligated to pay for taking on a loan should be at most be equal to 50% of the amount of money you're able to save every month. Why?

First, you must be able to save money every month because that implies you make more than what you spend for your living expenses. If you only make just enough for your needs or worse, less than that, you will not have any money to make your amortization payments. That means you can't afford to pay your debt when due.

When you're able to make more than you spend for living expenses, you need to set aside at least half for savings and emergencies. The other half is a good basis for comparing the required monthly amortization on a loan or debt you will take on. It should be considered as your "free" money, i.e., money that you can afford to spend any which way you want. If your monthly amortization is more than 50% of the amount of money you're able to save on a regular basis, it may keep you from saving enough money for the future and for emergencies.

Good and Bad Debts

Debt isn't inherently bad or good. What makes it bad or good is how it's used. Debt is bad under any of the following circumstances:

- Using proceeds of debt to buy something that you don't really need;
- Using proceeds of debt to buy things that depreciate in value; and
- Taking on debt the payment terms of which you can't afford.

Debt is only considered good under all of the following circumstances:

- Proceeds of debt will be used to buy something that you really need now but can't afford to pay for in one cash payment or for something that will make you more money than you'll have to pay; and
- The terms and conditions of which you can comfortably afford without straining your finances.

A good example of this is buying your house for your family. For most people, it's impossible to buy a house in cash. But it's possible to do so by taking on a home mortgage whose payment terms are very affordable and won't prevent you from providing for you and your family's needs such as clothing, food, and shelter, among others. A good rule of thumb is you should only take on a mortgage whose amortization payments are at least 50% less than the amount you're able to save every month. If it's more than said amount, it means you will have to cut down spending on some of your necessities, which isn't good.

If you take on debt whose payment terms you can't comfortably afford, your debt will grow bigger instead of diminishing over time. It can grow to a point when you may have to file for bankruptcy, which will do a lot of damage on your credit scores and ability to borrow money when you really need to. So, it's better to err on the side of caution and avoid borrowing money, saving it only for the times you really need to do it.

CHAPTER 7 – HOW TO GET OUT OF DEBT

The basic principle for getting out of debt is to ensure you spend less than you make. When you do, you will have excess funds for gradually paying off your debts. Otherwise, how can you make even a small dent on the money you owe to your creditors?

But this principle is easier said than done. For one, it's too general. How do you actually make more money than you spend so you can start paying off your debts? Once you have the money already, how do you go about paying off your debts? Here are practical things you can do that can collectively help you get out of debt sooner than you hope to.

Pay More than the Required Minimum

When you pay the minimum required payment every month on your credit card balance, it will take you way longer than you hoped to be able to pay off your debt completely. Why?

Assuming you don't add more to your current balance, minimum payments mean most of the money you pay will go to interest and only a small portion – if any – will be applied to the principal amount you owe. So, if only a small portion of your payments go to the principal balance, then it will take very long before you zero out that balance.

But if you pay more than the minimum requirement, you'll be able to pay off more of the principal balance, which can help you pay off your debt sooner. The greater the amount you pay in excess of the minimum required payment, the earlier you can pay off your debt completely.

For other debts payable on installment like student loans and mortgages, check first if your debt allows for prepayments without prepayment charges before you start paying off more than the amortization payments. If they do, check if it will be worth the charges.

The Snowball Method

The snowball method is a debt-payment strategy that involves 3 things:

- Listing down all your debts and arranging them from the smallest to the biggest balances;
- If you have excess funds for paying off more than the minimum payment requirements for all your debts, focus all the excess money on the smallest debt; and
- After you've completely paid off the smallest debt, focus all excess money for debt payments to the next smallest one and then the next…and so on until all your debts are paid.

The underlying principle here is this: when your smaller debts get paid off one at a time, you'll be able to free up more money to pay off the larger debts and accelerate their retirement. Over time, the money freed up from retiring smaller debts can "snowball" into bigger amounts that can accelerate payment of larger debts.

On a psychological note, prioritizing payment of smaller debts allow you to rack small but growing number of small victories that can encourage you more and more in your debt-retirement campaign. The more encouraged you feel, the higher your chances of persisting until you retire all your debts.

Side Hustles

While paying off debts with the snowball method can help you retire your debts faster, you can speed it up even more by making even more money available for it to accelerate the process! And one of the best and simplest ways to make more money available is to pick up a side hustle.

I believe everybody has a skill or talent that can be used for hustling extra money. And everybody includes you. Whether it's an innate ability to babysit, write blogs, edit videos, cook, cleaning houses, or mowing yards, you can make good extra money that you can throw into your debt payment efforts to accelerate the demise of your loan balances.

Some of the best websites to look for side hustles you can do on your spare time at your convenience are UpWork, Guru, and Fiverr. These sites are filled with a myriad number of side hustles like accounting work, graphic design, video editing, freelance writing, virtual assisting, and copywriting, among many others.

Look for Seasonal, Part-Time Work

During holiday seasons, many retail shops experience significantly higher than average foot traffic and consequently, sales. This compels them to hire extra hands to handle the substantial but temporary increase in customers and sales for those seasons. You can apply for such kinds of jobs on a temporary basis to have more money for accelerating your debt payments.

It's not just the holiday seasons that offer seasonal part-time work. Summer seasons usually see a spike in travel and tour-related business activities, which may require additional manpower for jobs like tour guiding. Spring season usually compels farms to hire additional greenhouse or field workers, among others.

Regardless of the season, there are available part-time jobs that you can snag to help generate more money for paying off your debts.

Live with a Skinny-Fit Budget

I use the term "skinny-fit" because skinny fit jeans are the epitome of tightness. And by a skinny-fit budget, I mean a budget that's practically bare-bones or a budget that cuts expenses so low that if you only budget for things that you really need to live and at the lowest possible price.

The skinny-fit budget is something that's undertaken only for as long as you pay off your debts and once done, you can revert back to a normal budget. The point of the skinny-fit budget is to free up as much money as possible for paying off and retiring personal debts as fast as possible.

Keep in mind that a skinny-fit budget looks different for every person. It's important that you're able to get an objective assessment of what your basic needs really are. The point is to have all of your basic needs met before paying off your debts, not to prioritize debts over your most basic needs. To summarize how things ought to be prioritized under a temporary skinny-fit budget:

1. Basic needs;
2. Debt payments; and
3. Non-essentials, i.e., recreation, etc.

Sell Your Unused Stuff

One of the quickest ways to get extra cash is to sell things you're no longer using. For this, you'll need to do take stock of all your personal belongings and real assets (a second car or a vacant property) and objectively determine which of them you're still using or may use on a regular basis within the next month or two. For those that you're not using anymore or won't be using anytime soon, you can sell them for extra debt-payment money.

If your neighborhood allows, hold a garage sale. If not, sell them on e-bay, Amazon, or other online stores. You can even advertise them for free on your Facebook or Instagram page or via paid Facebook and Instagram ads.

Negotiate with Your Debtors

If you find that your creditors' interest rates are very high, making it practically impossible to pay off your debts, consider giving them a call to negotiate for a much lower rate or even a suspension of it, if you're already unable to pay even the minimum amount and if your accounts are already way past due. You may not believe this but negotiating for a much lower interest rate is quite common in the financial services industry. Your chances of being able to successfully negotiate for a lower interest rate are much higher if you already have a history of being able to pay on time.

If your account's already way past due, calling up your creditors to negotiate for a suspension of interest and charges – or even their cancellation – and more affordable payment terms may also be a good idea. You see, doing this shows your creditors that you want to honor your debts – and them – and you need their help to make this happen. At the end of the day, creditors' only want to get paid back so by initiating negotiations with them, you can convince them that suspending interest and charges and granting you more favorable payment terms will be in their best economic interests.

Transfer Your Balance

If your creditors are adamant and refuse to give you more favorable payment terms, you may want to look into the possibility of transferring your debt balances to another financing or credit card company. There are companies that allow for 0% APR (annual percentage rate) for up to the first 1 ½ years for a balance transfer fee, which is usually around 3% of the balance to be transferred.

Use Your Bonuses or Increases

It's not impossible to come across "surprise" money during the year, e.g., performance bonuses, tax refunds, salary increases, inheritance, money gifts, etc. You can use these too for accelerating your debt payment efforts towards financial freedom. Combined with the snowball method, you can really push the pedal to the metal when it comes to paying off all your debts.

Ditch the Costly Habits

How much is a venti-sized serving of your favorite boutique skinny vanilla latte? Probably around $4.65 per, right? It may not amount to much if taken individually, but if you buy it every day going to work, you'd end up spending about $102[1] a month on the thing.

If you stop buying such expensive coffee and brew your own coffee at work using a French press, which I do, you can cut your caffeine-related expenses by 50% or more! That's at least $51 extra money you can add to debt payments.

Other very costly habits you can cut or seek cheaper and healthier alternatives for are eating commercially prepared foods for work-lunch, drinking and smoking. For lunch, why not prepare your meals in batches at home and just reheat and pack them for work? Not only is it much cheaper and can free up more funds for debt payments but it's also much healthier!

Flight, Not Fight

Everyone – you and I included – are prone to being tempted in one way or another. When it comes to living off a skinny-fit budget for accelerating debt payments, you must choose flight over fight when it comes to spending temptations. What do I mean by this?

There are 2 ways to handle temptations: flee (flight) from them or resist (fight) them. When you try to fight them, your chances of winning are very low. Why? They wouldn't be considered as temptations if they weren't very enticing or desirable. By exposing yourself to something you really like or want, you put yourself at risk of giving in.

When you choose to flee from temptations, your chances of not giving in are much higher because you remove yourself from things that trigger a behavior you want to change, such as spending habits. It's easier to avoid impulse spending when you don't go to malls or your favorite online shopping sites. But when you're already there, you may put yourself in a very steep uphill battle against impulse buying.

CONCLUSION

Thank you for buying this book. I hope that through this, you were able to learn a lot about mastering your personal finances, especially how to get and stay out of bad personal debts. But when it comes to money management, knowing's just half the battle. The other half is action, i.e., applying what you've learned.

So, I encourage you to start applying what you learned as soon as possible. The longer you procrastinate on it, the higher the risk that you won't do anything with what you learned. And if you don't do anything with it, you won't be able to reap the benefits associated with mastery of personal finances.

I also want to encourage you that as you apply what you learned, take baby steps. Apply one or two lessons at a time and when you've gotten them down to pat, apply one or two more and so on. That way, you don't get overwhelmed and you get to pile up many small personal finance victories that will give you increasing confidence and hope that you can master your lifestyle's financial aspect. And when you're able to master your personal finances, you can open more doors for mastering and enjoying all the other areas of your life.

Here's to your money management mastery, my friend! Cheers!

www.ingramcontent.com/pod-product-compliance
Lightning Source LLC
Chambersburg PA
CBHW051335220526
45468CB00004B/1654